[CODING YOUR PASSION™]

USING COMPUTER SCIENCE IN
FINANCIAL TECHNOLOGY
» CAREERS «

CARLA MOONEY

Rosen
YA™

New York

Published in 2018 by The Rosen Publishing Group, Inc.
29 East 21st Street, New York, NY 10010

Library of Congress Cataloging-in-Publication Data

Names: Mooney, Carla, 1970– author.
Title: Using computer science in financial technology careers / Carla Mooney.
Description: First edition. | New York : Rosen Publishing, 2018. | Series: Coding your passion | Includes bibliographical references and index.
Identifiers: LCCN 2016059460 | ISBN 9781508175131 (library bound)
Subjects: LCSH: Financial services industry—Information technology—Juvenile literature. | Computer science—Vocational guidance—Juvenile literature. | Finance—Vocational guidance—Juvenile literature.
Classification: LCC HG173 .M6358 2018 | DDC 332.1/70285—dc23
LC record available at https://lccn.loc.gov/2016059460

Manufactured in China

CONTENTS

INTRODUCTION

Brothers John and Patrick Collison learned to program code growing up in Ireland. They practiced their coding skills building iPhone apps and web services. After high school, the brothers traveled to the United States for college. Patrick enrolled at the Massachusetts Institute of Technology (MIT) while John attended Harvard University.

During his freshman year at MIT, Patrick founded a small tech company called Auctomatic, which built applications for eBay sellers. Ten months after incorporating his company, in 2008, nineteen-year-old Patrick sold the business to Live Current Media for $5 million.

While working at Auctomatic, Patrick continued to develop apps and platforms for other clients. He talked to John about why it was so hard to accept payment on the web. When Patrick wanted to charge people for apps he built, he had to go to the bank and file paperwork that needed to be approved. "And it would take sort of weeks for this approval process to happen. And it just seemed sort of like this crazy mismatch," says Patrick, according to an article on the CBS News website.

Patrick and John began working on a solution to make the payment process much simpler. They created software that allows individuals and

John Collison, cofounder and president of the payment processing fintech company Stripe, listens intently during an international technology conference in Hong Kong, China, in 2015.

businesses to instantly accept payments online. For six months, they developed their idea, showed it to friends, and watched how people interacted with it. They used the feedback they received to tweak and adjust their technology.

At first, the brothers were not sure if there was a market for their technology or if they could provide the right user experience. However, within six months, they realized their idea had great potential. By the fall of 2010, both John and Patrick worked full-time on their start-up, which they named Stripe.

With Stripe, web developers integrate payment processing into a website. They do not have to register and maintain a merchant account with a bank. For initial transactions, Stripe takes two days to profile businesses and protect against fraud. The process is much faster than traditional credit card or bank payment processing. Once the transaction is verified, Stripe transfers money directly into the payee's bank account. "We want to free businesses from just selling via credit cards, you know, to people who hold bank accounts, and instead, enable people to purchase online no matter what it is that they use, bank account or no," says Patrick in the same article.

In a few short years, Stripe has grown tremendously. By 2016, the San Francisco–based company had 480 employees and an investment valuation around $5 billion. Stripe makes money by collecting a swipe fee of 2.9 percent and 30 cents for every transaction it processes. Since its launch, Stripe has processed billions of dollars' work of transactions for hundreds of thousands of companies.

The combination of finance and technology has become an industry called "fintech." Thousands of companies are working to make banking, investing, and other financial activities easier, faster, and increasingly mobile. Fintech platforms match borrowers and lenders. Algorithms help people with financial planning. And other technologies like Stripe are revolutionizing the way payments are made.

Investors recognize the potential of fintech. They have poured over $20 billion into financial technology and companies.

Fintech is changing the way people bank, pay for goods, invest their money, and more. The rise of fintech is also opening the door to new businesses and opportunities. People work in fintech all over the world, from London to San Francisco. There are many different fintech career specialties that students can pursue. Fintech companies employ software programmers, developers, data scientists, security engineers, marketing professionals, and more. With so many opportunities, fintech careers can fit many backgrounds and interests.

CHAPTER ONE

WHAT IS FINTECH?

Financial technology, or fintech, is a growing industry made up of companies that create and use technology to provide financial services. Fintech has changed the way companies do business and consumers handle their financial affairs. It has made financial services more effective and efficient.

In many cases, fintech companies are small start-ups that are taking the place of larger financial corporations. Fintech start-ups have increased from about one thousand in 2005 to over twelve thousand in 2016. These companies have created cutting-edge technology to provide financial services. They operate more efficiently and cheaply than traditional banks. Many fintech firms offer the same traditional services as banks, from payment processing to lending. At the same time, several large financial companies have recognized the need to keep up with financial technology. Many are adding their own fintech solutions to improve their business and customer service.

Tech entrepreneurs meet and network at Rise London, a business accelerator that helps to launch new start-up fintech companies by providing office space and facilities.

In recent years, investment in fintech has skyrocketed. According to Boston Consulting Group, total fintech funding reached $78.6 billion in 2016. Companies in North America, Europe, and Asia are all part of the fintech movement. And fintech is only expected to grow in the future. According to a 2015 report by TransferWise, a fintech lending company, the number of consumers using fintech for at least one financial service is expected to double within five years.

HOW THE FINTECH BOOM STARTED

In the early years, financial technology was primarily used by big businesses. Large database solutions stored and protected company information. A company's staff was trained on how to use the databases. There was little interaction between the technology and consumers.

In 2008, the world economy faced its biggest crisis since the Great Depression of the 1930s. In the United States, a housing bubble inflated the prices of homes across the country. After peaking in early 2006, housing prices began to fall in late 2006 and 2007. People who had taken out loans on their homes found themselves unable to make mortgage payments or pay skyrocketing interest rates. Many defaulted on their loans. Mortgage lenders, investment banks, and other financial institutions that had invested in these loans lost money. Some large mortgage lenders and investment banks went out of business or were purchased by other companies. The federal government was forced to bail out Fannie Mae and Freddie Mac, two government institutions created to buy mortgages and provide mortgage lenders with more money to lend.

The financial crisis spread beyond the mortgage and housing industries. Banks stopped making loans to companies that relied on credit, such as the American auto industry. Share prices of companies dropped around the world. By the end of 2008, a deep recession had spread through most of the world.

Fannie Mae is the largest US home funding company. After the housing bubble crashed in late 2006 and 2007, the federal government bailed out Fannie Mae so that the company would not fail.

The crisis caused many people to lose faith in traditional banking and financial systems. They realized finance and banking systems needed innovation. Fintech emerged as a way to serve customer needs without the formality and regulation of banks. It also made the banking system more efficient.

The boom of mobile technology also gave a boost to fintech. Armed with smartphones, consumers were no longer tethered to a specific location or desktop computer. They wanted to be able to access financial systems on the go, wherever and whenever they wanted. Traditional banking systems were not designed for mobile use and interaction with consumers. Instead, fintech solutions emerged for mobile users.

REINVENTING BANKING TECHNOLOGY

In the past, only a bank could compete with another bank. With financial technology, there is no need for a central bank. Each part of the banking experience can be built independently by fintech companies.

Fintech companies are reinventing the technology behind all types of financial services, from lending and payments to billing, wealth management, personal finance, and digital currency. Fintech is replacing outdated systems in big investment banks with better-designed and more intuitive web-based platforms that both the bank and its customers can use. "When we look at large universal banks, they have 400 to 500 core activities or processes," says Fritz Nauck, a McKinsey & Company director, in an article on Bloomberg.com. "Over two-thirds don't touch the client at all. While not all that stuff can be digitized or automated overnight, a lot of those steps certainly can be, so we think there is a large opportunity to get more productive."

Many small start-up companies are creating financial technology. According to a December 2014 report by consulting firm McKinsey & Company, there are more than twelve thousand fintech start-ups across the United States. Many are located in Silicon Valley, California, or New York City.

FINANCIAL TECHNOLOGY FOR ENTREPRENEURS AND CONSUMERS

Fintech is doing more than creating technology for big commercial and investment banks. Many fintech companies are creating products that can be used by the average consumer. Using the wide reach of the internet, they have created technology for consumers in areas such as personal investing, wealth management, and lending. These tools can be used by virtually anyone.

Many new companies that create technology for the financial industry are located in New York City's Financial District.

For entrepreneurs, fintech has made it easier than ever to set up and do business. To get a loan, new businesses no longer have to go to a traditional bank. Peer-to-peer lending or crowdsourcing enable them to get funding from anywhere in the world. Using the internet, entrepreneurs can pitch their business idea to people located worldwide. Instead of waiting for months, they can receive their funding in only a few weeks. Fintech can also help companies do business and lower costs. For example, fintech platforms have simplified transferring money from one country to another. Companies such as TransferWise allow small firms and individuals to transfer money overseas much faster and cheaper than ever. When companies using fintech to save money on costs, they can pass along these savings to customers.

With mobile devices, people are always online. They want to access information and data at any time or place. New fintech apps and platforms allow the average person to handle their financial matters easily and conveniently on the go. Companies like Venmo allow people to exchange money over mobile devices for almost anything.

They can use a smartphone to pay rent or buy theater tickets. Companies like Square make it easier for small stores and entrepreneurs to accept credit card payments on a smartphone or tablet. Other companies have created tools for people to check online bank accounts, transfer money between accounts, use online budgeting tools, and even set up online investment portfolios.

WORKING IN FINTECH

People interested in fintech careers have many options. They can work for a variety of companies,

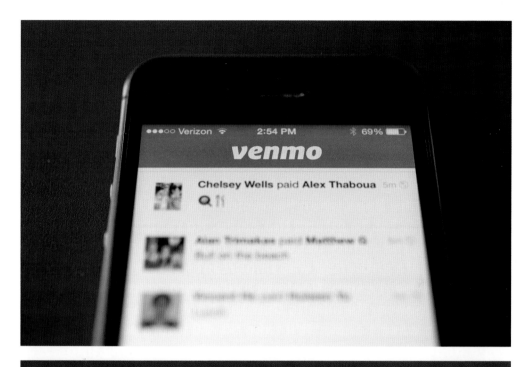

Using the mobile-payment app Venmo, tech-savvy smartphone users can connect to their bank and credit card accounts to send payments and receive money from friends.

from small start-ups to large corporations. In both environments, fintech professionals often work as part of a cross-functional team. Team members come from different departments and have different roles.

In all companies, having strong computer science skills is essential for most fintech careers. Many people working in fintech have a computer science degree. A few have degrees in math, physics, or engineering. No matter their degree, people working in fintech need to have knowledge of basic financial systems and web technology. Knowledge

CODING BOOT CAMP

Some people, like banker Josh Panknin, decide to attend a coding boot camp to get up to speed on the coding needed in fintech. Panknin worked at Deutsche Bank when he decided to take time off from his job to attend the camp. He realized that having the ability to code and automate analysis and data gathering was important in finance. Prior to the boot camp, Panknin had no programming experience. He admits that the boot camp–style program wasn't easy. "It'll take 60–80 hours per week depending on your level of experience coming into the course and how quickly you can grasp the concepts. The material isn't just about typing code into the computer, it's about thinking logically and solving problems using code. So sometimes a single problem can take an entire day (or two days in my case), but each time the process gets quicker and you get better," he says in an article on Techday.com. After he finishes the program, Panknin plans to either seek a job in fintech or go back to finance armed with programming skills to make him more efficient.

Coding boot camps can run for a few weeks to a few months. They can meet in person or online. Some people who enroll in coding boot camps have no previous programming skills. Others are professional

developers who want to keep up to date on the latest programming languages. Supporters say that boot camps allow coders to develop the skills they need in a short amount of time. Critics point out that the camps are often expensive and there is no guarantee a person will find a high-paying job afterward.

of programming languages such as Java, JavaScript, C++, and C# are valuable. Many investment banks and other financial institutions already use these programming languages, which can be adapted for use in front-end web design.

JavaScript is primarily used to build websites and create a better user experience. It is also an essential skill for building Android apps. Many companies have said that the need for JavaScript developers is much greater than the number of qualified candidates. C++ and C# are programming languages that are useful in fintech. Fintech professionals often use C++ and C# to create software when there is a high volume of trading transactions or when a large amount of data needs quick processing. Like Java, C# can also be used in simulation or modeling tools. Python is another common programming language used in fintech platforms. Programmers use Python to build analytic tools and develop models. Knowing R language is another helpful skill in fintech. This software is used for calculations and data analysis.

In addition to technical skills, the ability to work well together and communicate is critical for most fintech careers. "Having the ability to collaborate and work across various teams, locations and time zones is key to achieving common goals and objectives. It is also really important to be able to motivate and inspire those you work with," says Mai Clark, a program manager in Royal Bank of Scotland's IT team in an article on efinancialcareers.com.

In addition, many companies are looking for candidates that can problem solve and communicate well with others. "We're looking for people who can think logically and laterally—you need to be able to solve problems," says Scott Marcar, head of IT infrastructure at Deutsche Bank in the same article. "We're looking for innovators who can think outside the box. And we're looking for communicators—the ability to communicate both internally and externally is critical. If you're strong in each of these three things, you will have a very strong application."

PURSUING A CAREER IN FINTECH

People who are interested in a fintech career should take classes to give them solid technical computer and programming skills. Some people choose to get a computer-related degree from a four-year college or university. Others who have degrees in another field attend special coding boot camps or fintech-focused graduate programs.

In addition to taking classes, people interested in a fintech career can take other steps to learn more about the industry. Joining a college finance or business society can help a person learn more about financial technology and make contacts in the industry. Some banks and start-up companies offer internships to students. Internships give students the experience of working for a particular company or industry. Reading newspapers and other business and technology publications can help students keep up to date on the latest in finance and technology.

CHAPTER TWO

CREATING PAYMENT SYSTEMS

Payment processing is one of the hottest areas in fintech. Fintech companies are using cutting-edge technology to transform how transactions are initiated and processed. Using technology, they are making the payment process simpler. "This is about creating a wide, and inclusive, alternative to cash and checks for everyone," says Paul Finch, chief executive of the bank network operator Early Warning Services in an article on Reuters.com.

ONLINE PAYMENTS

Technology has created new ways to pay, such as online payments and mobile wallets. With online payments, a person can send payment to another person with just a few clicks of a mouse or swipes on a smartphone. These systems are website- or

As more people shop online, financial technology has created online payment systems like PayPal. These systems allow users to pay for purchases online without using checks or cash.

app-based, which means that a person does not have to install software or buy special equipment to use them. Online payment systems can be accessed from any device connected to the internet. Founded in 1998, PayPal is one of the first and most successful online payment systems.

For businesses, companies like Square make it easier to accept credit card payments. Founded in 2009, Square allows vendors to accept credit card payments with the Square Register app. Businesses can also use a tiny physical card reader that attaches to the headphone jack of any smartphone to accept credit card payments. They can also use a tablet-based terminal stand instead of other checkout systems or a wireless checkout station that works with Apple Pay. Square even makes an app that allows consumers to transfer money between people easily, such as when two friends split a bill at a restaurant.

Stripe is another fintech company that makes it easier for small businesses to accept credit card payments online. Founded in 2010, Stripe is a web application that allows vendors to accept credit card payment through their websites. Using Stripe, web developers can add payment processing to a vendor's website without having to register and maintain a merchant account, a special bank account that allows the merchant to accept credit card payments. Developers can customize the Stripe app for their business's specific payment needs.

INTERNATIONAL MONEY TRANSFERS

Even international money transfers have become easier with technology. Companies such as TransferWise send money internationally easier, faster, and cheaper than traditional methods. TransferWise uses sophisticated peer-to-peer software to match payments going overseas with payments going the opposite direction. The money being sent never actually leaves the country. TransferWise simply reroutes it to someone who is being sent a similar amount from overseas.

Taavet Hinrikus (*pictured*) speaks at a global technology conference. He is the cofounder and CFO of TransferWise, a fintech company that allows users to send and receive money internationally.

The foreign recipient receives funds from someone trying to send money out of their own country. But TransferWise's customers never have to deal with this complex payment matching. They simply send and receive funds.

MOBILE WALLETS

For consumers, the rapid increase in smartphone use around the world is driving innovation in mobile wallet technology. Mobile wallets offer consumers a new way to pay for the goods they purchase. A mobile wallet is basically a digital version of a traditional wallet that a person would carry in his or her purse or pocket. Mobile wallets can hold digital information about credit and debit cards, store coupons and loyalty programs, and other personal information.

Mobile wallets such as Apple Pay, Google Wallet, and MobiKwik allow consumers to make payments using their mobile phones. A mobile wallet carries credit card or debit card information in digital form. The digital information might be a number, a digital certificate, a QR code, or something else. It is linked to the consumer's bank or credit card information. Instead of pulling out a credit card or cash to make a payment, consumers can simply pay with their smartphone, tablet, or smartwatch. To do so, they open an app on their phone and enter a PIN, password, or fingerprint to authorize the payment. The app communicates with the vendor's mobile wallet payment terminal.

Because mobile wallets provide access to financial accounts and personal information, security is an important issue. Some companies are working on the use of biometric data to authorize payments. They are testing the use of fingerprints, voices, irises, and faces to authorize payments. Tokenization is another security method being tested. With tokenization, a consumer's credit card details are translated into temporary tokens. This allows mobile payments to be authorized without disclosing the related credit card information to the recipient.

WORKING AS A SOFTWARE DEVELOPER

Software developers design computer programs. Some create the applications that allow people to perform specific tasks on a computer or a mobile device. Others work on the systems that run the devices and computer networks. In the fintech payments sector, software developers create the applications and platforms needed to run payment processing systems and other financial technology.

A student interested in becoming a software developer for the fintech industry practices writing code while in a class to learn a new programming language.

Typically, software developers design, test, and develop software that meets customer needs. Often, they begin by talking with customers to see what they need and how they plan to use the software. Through these discussions and other research, software developers determine the core functions required in the software program. They must also determine other user requirements, such as security and performance. With this information, developers design the program.

They give detailed instructions to programmers, who write and test the program code. In some companies, software developers write the code themselves. If the resulting application does not work as intended, software developers tweak the design to fix the problems. After the application is released, developers may continue to improve it with upgrades and maintenance.

Software developers can specialize in different areas. Applications software developers design computer applications such as games or word processing programs. They create custom software for individual clients. They also create applications that can be used over the internet. Systems software developers create the systems that keep a company's computers working properly. They develop operating systems and system interfaces, which allow users to interact with a computer, mobile device, or other electronic system. Developers who supervise a software project from planning through implementation are sometimes called information technology project managers.

LEARNING THROUGH INTERNSHIP

In the summer of 2013, Katelyn Lesse worked as a software engineering intern at Betterment, a fin-tech company that uses technology to help people invest and manage their money. Lesse was in college at Princeton University, majoring in computer science. During the internship, Lesse created five visual dashboards that showed different data on how the company was performing. She says that the experience was very challenging but also invaluable for her career. She needed to learn a lot of computer languages on the job. "The different pieces in the structure of a web app are usually written in different computer languages...Accessing the database requires knowledge of SQL, a lot of scripts are written in Python, front end structure and design is written in HTML and CSS, and front end animation is written in JavaScript. In order to effectively work on multiple pieces of an app, an engineer needs to be fluent in multiple different languages...My experience this summer has been invaluable, and I will be returning to school with a brand new view on software development and what a career in this awesome field will be like," she says in an article on Betterment.com.

HOW TO BECOME A SOFTWARE DEVELOPER

Most software developers have at least a bachelor's degree in computer science, software engineering, or a related field from a four-year college or university. Although not all developers write code, students should also take classes to develop strong software computer programming skills. Even after they graduate from college, software developers must continue to develop their computer skills and stay current on new tools and programming languages. Many students complete an internship at a software company to gain hands-on experience in software development. Some people enter the field by first working as computer programmers. As they gain experience, they take on more responsibility and can eventually become software developers.

In addition to strong computer skills, several additional skills are important for people working as software developers. Software developers in the fintech industry should also have some knowledge of finance so that they can understand their company's and customers' needs. Developers should also be creative, have good analytical skills, and be detail oriented. A good software developer can analyze customer needs and develop a creative solution to meet those needs. Developers should also have excellent communication and interpersonal skills. Many developers work closely with others on a team.

They must be able to communicate effectively with team members. Also, developers often have to explain how the software works to customers.

JOB OUTLOOK

The job outlook for software developers is strong. According to the Bureau of Labor Statistics' *Occupational Outlook Handbook*, employment of software developers is projected to grow 17 percent from 2014 to 2024. This rate of growth is much faster than the average of all occupations. The main driver behind

A software developer works at his computer station. He is concentrating on customizing an online payment system for his client, a retail company that sells made-to-order mountain bikes.

this employment growth is an increasing demand for computer software. In addition, the need for new applications on mobile devices will also increase the demand for application software developers. Systems developers will see new job opportunities as the number of products that use software increases.

Concerns over security could result in the need for more security software to protect computer networks and applications, particularly in the fintech industry. In addition, as more fintech applications are being offered over the internet, opportunities to customize these applications for individual business and consumer needs will increase the need for software developers. Candidates who have strong skills in the most up-to-date programming tools and languages will have the best prospects for landing a good software development job in the fintech industry.

CHAPTER THREE

OPENING UP LENDING

For many years, banks were the only place a person could get a loan. The process typically took a long time. People without the best credit were often turned away or charged very high interest rates. Fintech has created a new way for people to borrow and lend money. With online lending, people can apply for a loan by filling out a simple online application. Approval can take only a few hours. They can get different types of loans, from personal loans to refinancing student debt.

PEER-TO-PEER LENDING

One type of online lending is peer-to-peer (P2P) lending. P2P platforms operate much differently than traditional banks. The platform does not lend its own money. Instead, it matches borrowers and lenders over the internet. On websites like Prosper Marketplace

On December 11, 2014, Lending Club, a peer-to-peer online lending platform, became a public company and began trading its stock on the New York Stock Exchange.

and Lending Club, borrowers complete a simple online application. The companies use technology and software to quickly assess risk, determine a credit rating, and assign appropriate interest rates. People with money to lend read their information and credit scores and decide whether or not to make the loan. Lenders can also participate in pools of loans, which limits their risk to any one loan.

The entire online lending process cuts out the middleman—the banks. In doing so, borrowers usually pay a lower interest rate than they would on credit card debt or an unsecured loan. Lenders earn higher returns than they would in a savings account or a certificate of deposit. In return, lenders take on more risk. The P2P platform makes money on the origination fees it charges borrowers and from service fees it charges to lenders.

P2P platforms rely on technology to perform innovative credit modeling and data analysis to evaluate borrowers. Some P2P platforms also offer automated loan selection in which investors determine certain criteria for loans they want to make. The system automatically filters and finds suitable loans for them.

The popularity of P2P lending is soaring. According to a Federal Reserve Bank of Cleveland report, P2P interest rates are often lower than credit card rates for most borrowers. This combined with a user-friendly and efficient lending platform has attracted borrowers and lenders alike. In 2014, United States P2P platforms issued approximately $5.5 billion in loans. That number could soar to $150 billion or higher by 2025 according to a report prepared by PricewaterhouseCoopers. While P2P platforms primarily started out as a way for people to get a small-dollar personal loan, the model is expanding into mortgages and other types of secured loans.

CROWDFUNDING

Fintech has also made raising money for a creative idea or new business venture easier. Crowdfunding websites or platforms allow individuals and business owners to raise funds for any type of project. They give users access to a large number of potential investors. Sites such as GoFundMe, Kickstarter, and Indiegogo are used by people worldwide to fund a variety of projects. Some people might use a crowdfunding site to raise money to help a family that is facing unexpected medical bills. Some people use crowdfunding sites to finance artistic projects, such as a movie or a music album.

Other people use crowdfunding to finance a new business. Prior to the internet, it was difficult to match entrepreneurs and potential investors. It took a lot of

The Cats Not Ads campaign replaced dozens of advertisements in this London subway station with pictures of cats. The campaign was funded through Kickstarter.

time and resources to network and negotiate a deal. Also, traditional investment minimums often excluded smaller potential investors. Fintech's crowdfunding solutions have made this process much easier. Equity crowdfunding is the practice of investing in an early-stage company in exchange for shares in that company. Shareholders own part of the company and profit if the company does well. If the company fails, however, the shareholders can lose some or all of their investment.

On platforms such as Fundable and Circle Up, investors can search for investment opportunities, review a company's information, and make a decision about whether or not to invest. Also, fintech platforms allow investors to invest as little as $10 in a company or product they support. With low barriers to entry, entrepreneurs can raise money from friends, family, angel investors, and others. Before fintech, only insiders had the chance to invest early in companies with enormous potential. With fintech platforms, average people can buy into the next big company before it becomes a public company listed on the stock exchanges.

The Pebble smartwatch is one example of a crowdfunding success. The Pebble smartwatch works with apps on a person's smartphone to give notification of important calls, emails, or other alerts right on the watch's face display. In only twenty-eight hours, Pebble raised $1 million in crowdfunding. Eventually, the company raised more than $10 million for its ideas.

WORKING AS A DATA SCIENTIST

Fintech lending platforms are data-driven businesses. They need data scientists to make sense of all the data they receive and put it into a useful and understandable format. They use their skills in math, statistics, and computer science to gather and organize enormous amounts of data. Then they use analytical skills and industry knowledge to find solutions for the business. Data scientists write algorithms to analyze large amounts of data. They build predictive models to assess a person's creditworthiness. They build software to help a company make

Using data from many sources, a data scientist builds a computer algorithm to analyze information.

decisions about interest rates, credit, funding, and other areas.

Each day, data scientists may be asked to perform a variety of tasks. They might conduct research on industry questions. They can extract huge volumes of data from a variety of sources. They may operate sophisticated analytics programs and statistical methods to prepare data for predictive modeling. They use software programs to cleanse data and eliminate irrelevant information. They will examine the data from different perspectives to identify trends, opportunities, and weaknesses. They will use computer skills to create algorithms to solve problems and build tools to automate work. They will also prepare reports that communicate their findings and results for management.

Some jobs will focus more on data analytics— collecting, processing statistical analyses of data, and using the information to answer questions and solve problems. Other jobs require data scientists to build massive databases for big data information. They develop, build, test, and maintain these databases and data processing systems. Once these systems are built, data scientists can use them to access specific data for analysis.

As data scientists gain more experience, their responsibilities often change. A person new to the job might spend most of the day cleaning data and preparing it for analysis. A more senior data scientist may spend more time designing big data projects or creating new company products.

WHAT IS AN ALGORITHM?

Data scientists frequently write algorithms in their jobs. An algorithm is a set of directions that tells a computer what steps to take to complete a specific task. The algorithm tells the computer, step by step, exactly what the data scientist wants it to do. When the data scientist runs the program, the computer performs each step, in order. In computer programming, there are also different ways, or algorithms, to accomplish a task. Each algorithm has advantages and disadvantages. A data scientist must decide which algorithm is right to use in a certain set of circumstances.

HOW TO BECOME A DATA SCIENTIST

Most data scientists have a master's degree or PhD, in addition to a bachelor's degree. They often major in areas such as mathematics, statistics, or computer science. Taking courses in math and statistics prepares students to work in data scientist jobs. These courses can help students develop the technical skills they will need in linear algebra, calculus, probability, statistical hypothesis testing, and summary statistics. In addition, students should take courses to develop machine-learning tools and techniques.

Two college students work together to practice database and other computer skills that will be essential in a career as a data scientist.

Computer science skills are critical for data scientists. Potential employees need to be able to work with data through data mining, cleaning and munging, and data visualization. They should also be proficient in programming languages such as Python, C/C++, Java, and Perl. They should be skilled in working with SQL databases and database querying languages. In addition, data scientists should develop skills to work with cloud tools such as Amazon S3. Because the computer science environment is always changing, data scientists must continue to develop new computer skills and stay current on new tools and programming languages.

In addition to strong technical skills, several additional skills are important for people working as data scientists. Data scientists in the fintech industry should have a working knowledge of finance so that they can understand their company's and customers' needs. Problem-solving skills are also important because data scientists have to create new ways of looking at and analyzing data. Data scientists should have excellent communication and interpersonal skills. Many data scientists work closely with others in a team. The work is often spread among team members, and the ability to work well with others and communicate is essential. In addition, data scientists must be able to communicate effectively with management and others who may not have a technical background.

JOB OUTLOOK

The job outlook for data scientists is very good. According to the Bureau of Labor Statistics' *Occupational Outlook Handbook*, employment of computer and information research scientists is projected to grow 11 percent from 2014 to 2024. This rate of growth is faster than the average for all occupations. In fintech, this growth is driven by the rapid increase in data collection by companies and a resulting increased need for data-mining services. Computer data scientists will be needed to write algorithms to help fintech businesses understand large amounts of data. With this information, companies can understand their customers better.

Many companies report difficulty finding these highly skilled workers. Therefore, the job prospects for data scientists are good. Candidates who have strong technical and analytical skills in the most up-to-date programming tools and languages will have the best prospects for landing a good data scientist job in the fintech industry.

CHAPTER FOUR

TOOLS FOR WEALTH MANAGEMENT AND PERSONAL FINANCE

In the areas of wealth management and personal finance, fintech has leveled the playing field for the average person. Before fintech, many investment advisory services were limited to people with bank accounts over a certain dollar amount. Now, technology and data have opened those services to everyone. The average person can use online tools and apps to research and manage investments as well as plan and budget personal finances. User-friendly platforms allow people to be more involved in investment and personal finance.

ROBO ADVISERS

Robo advisers are online investment services that replace a traditional human adviser. Investors answer a series of questions online. With this information, the

Investors review and analyze investment charts and portfolio allocations. These reports have been created by robo advisers, online investment services that replace traditional human advisers.

robo adviser uses algorithms to create an investment plan. The plan determines the portfolio allocation for each person. Portfolio allocation takes the money a person wants to invest and balances it between different types of investments, such as stocks, fixed-income securities, and cash. Each type of investment has a different amount of risk associated with it and a different expected return. "Robo advising takes what historically required a meeting with a person in an office and moves it to an automated or crowd-enabled, mobile-enabled device, making the experience much more familiar and less intimidating," says Joy Schoffler, executive board member for the Fintech Professional Association in an article on Goodcall.com. "As millennials begin to plan for their retirement futures, it's likely that a majority of investments will be made without ever talking to a person."

Experts say that financial technology is a good fit for investment services because it does not require much involvement to create a basic financial plan based on risk tolerance and the amount of time available for investing. "There are certain aspects of financial planning and management that can easily be put in an app and done via an algorithm," says Lucila Williams, president and founder of LOTUS Financial Partners, in the same article. "These apps and websites are reaching a generation of people at an asset level that the average financial advisor can't."

Online robo advisers are available through several platforms, such as Wealthfront and Betterment. These platforms expand the number of people entering the investing market by reducing account minimums and making it simple for investors. They also reduce the fees charged by traditional financial advisers. For example, Wealthfront requires only $500 to open an account. It manages an investor's first $10,000 free and charges a small annual fee of .25% for amounts over $10,000.

Traditional investment companies are also adopting digital investment tools. Established asset managers, wealth management companies, and insurance companies are jumping on the technology trends. These players are building, buying, and partnering with robo advising technologies. For example, traditional financial advisers such as Vanguard and Schwab have launched robo adviser platforms for customers. These platforms include an option for customers to interact with a human if they want.

PERSONAL FINANCE AND SAVINGS

Most banks offer online banking technology and mobile apps. Customers can view account activity, transfer money, and pay bills online. With online banking technology, customers have access to their

With online banking technology, a man can sit on his couch at home and use his laptop to pay bills, transfer money, and check his bank account balances online.

accounts from any place, at any time, as long as they have an internet connection and a mobile device.

Beyond banking, technology is also helping people budget and save money. Budgeting apps and platforms sync with a person's financial accounts to track spending and savings in real time. These apps allow users to track spending in different categories and send notifications if a user exceeds his or her budget. They can also perform analyses to determine where a person spends money. Other apps make it easy to save. Some services use algorithms to figure out how much a user can afford to save each month and automatically transfer money to a savings account.

Level Money is a personal finance app. Cofounder Jake Fuentes says that when he graduated from college, he had $33,000 in student loan debt and $11,000 in credit card debt. He was not satisfied with the financial tools available to him to help manage his debt. "We're surrounded by money management tools that for lots of people are way too complicated. We take all that information and simplify it down to its essence," he says on Fintechranking.com. Instead of being complicated, Fuentes believes that managing money should be as simple as opening a wallet and seeing how much cash is left. With Level Money, Fuentes attempted to do this. The app connects a user's bank accounts, reviews expenses, and recommends a savings rate. It also advises users how much money they have left to spend. For example, if a user walks into a store, the app might send a notification that he or she has $22 left to spend for the day and $72 for the week. Since its launch in October 2013, the app has been used by about 750,000 people and has helped users manage over $12 billion in transactions.

WORKING AS A WEB DEVELOPER IN FINTECH

Many fintech platforms in wealth management, personal finance, and more rely on websites to interact with users. Web developers design and create these websites. They are responsible for the sites' appearance and technical features. These include the sites' performance or speed and their capacity, which is the amount of user traffic they can handle. Some web developers also create content for sites.

In a typical day, web developers might meet with clients or coworkers to talk about the function and design of a website. They write code for websites, often using programming languages such as HTML or XML. They create and test applications for the site. They work with other team members and designers to determine a site's information, graphics, and layout. They incorporate graphics, audio, and video into the site. Once the site is up and running, web developers monitor traffic, make adjustments or additions as necessary, and troubleshoot any problems.

Web developers customize websites to a customer's or company's needs. Different types of websites need different applications to work correctly.

A web developer uses HTML to customize a customer's website. He relies on features such as integrated payment processing, online shopping carts, customer feedback systems, and more.

For example, a personal finance site should have an integrated budgeting application. Working with the rest of the product development team, the web developer determines which applications and design work best for the site.

While some web developers handle every part of a website's construction, from design to maintenance, others specialize in certain areas. Back-end web developers focus on how a site operates. They oversee the website's technical construction. They create the site's basic framework and make sure that it works as designed. Back-end developers also determine the process for adding new pages and information to the website. In contrast, front-end web developers focus more on how a site looks and how users interact with it. They create layouts and integrate graphics, applications, and other content. Front-end developers often write web programs in computer languages such as HTML or JavaScript. Once a website is up and running, webmasters maintain and update it.

HOW TO BECOME A WEB DEVELOPER

Most web developers have at least an associate's degree in web design or a related field. For more technical jobs, some employers want employees to have at least a bachelor's degree in computer science, programming, or a related field. Taking courses in graphic design can also be helpful, especially if the web developer will be involved in creating a website's visual appearance.

Web developers should have strong technical and web-programming skills. They must be proficient in HTML, the markup language for making web pages. Developers should also have strong technical skills in other programming languages such as JavaScript and CSS and be able to work with multimedia publishing tools such as Flash. Because the computer science environment is always changing, web developers must continue to develop new computer skills and stay current on new tools and programming languages.

In addition to strong technical skills, web developers should also have several other qualities and skills to be successful. Because web developers often spend a lot of time at a computer, writing detailed code for hours, the ability to concentrate and focus on small details is extremely important. A tiny error in the HTML code could cause an entire webpage to stop working. Successful web developers are often very creative people, which can help them

A web developer works late into the night to add new features to a client's website and meet the upcoming project deadline.

design a website's appearance and make sure it is innovative and fresh. Web developers in the fintech industry should also have a knowledge of finance so that they can understand their company's and customers' needs. Web developers should also have excellent communication and interpersonal skills. Many web developers work closely with others in a team. The work is often spread among team members, and the ability to work well with others and communicate is essential. In addition, web developers must be able to communicate effectively with management and others who may not have a technical background.

HTML: THE WEB'S LANGUAGE

Web developers know how to use HTML coding to build websites. HTML stands for "hypertext markup language." Developed by scientist Tim Berners-Lee in 1990, it is the language used to create web pages that can be displayed in a web browser. HTML uses tags to mark blocks of text on a page. One of the most common HTML tags used is the <strong> or bold tag. It is used to mark text that should be bolded. For example, <strong>this is bold text</strong>.

JOB OUTLOOK

The job outlook for web developers is very good. According to the Bureau of Labor Statistics' *Occupational Outlook Handbook*, employment of web developers is projected to grow 27 percent from 2014 to 2024. This rate of growth is much faster than the average of all occupations. In fintech, this growth is driven by the rapid increase in online platforms and services for consumers. As finance companies expand their online offerings, demand for web developers will continue to increase. In addition, the increasing use of mobile devices will also increase the number of opportunities, as developers will be needed to create sites that work on mobile devices and multiple screen sizes.

Although some web developer jobs may be moved to other countries with lower wages, the cost to manage foreign workers can offset any wage savings. In addition, web developers often need to be familiar with cultural nuances as they build and design webpages. For these reasons, many companies prefer to hire local web developers. Candidates who have strong technical skills and knowledge of multiple programming languages and digital multimedia tools will have the best opportunities for working as web developers in the fintech industry.

CHAPTER FIVE

DIGITAL CURRENCY

D igital currencies, or cryptocurrencies, might one day change the way people pay for goods and services online. A cryptocurrency is a virtual currency that uses cryptography or codes for security. Digital currencies allow users to exchange online credits for goods and services. They are not issued by any central bank or authority.

BITCOIN

Emerging in 2009, the Bitcoin is one of the most well-known digital currencies. It was developed by an anonymous person or group known as Satoshi Nakamoto. Bitcoin is a cryptocurrency that uses strong encryption algorithms to secure transactions. Bitcoin users have pseudonyms to hide their identities. Users can buy Bitcoins from online exchanges and brokerages.

A man buys Bitcoins at the first Bitcoin ATM in Tel Aviv. Bitcoin is a digital cryptocurrency that uses strong encryption algorithms to secure transactions.

They assign the Bitcoins to a personal wallet, which is like an online account. Bitcoins are not like physical currency. There is nothing to hold. Instead, Bitcoins are simple entries in a public ledger known as the blockchain. The blockchain records Bitcoin balances and transfers amounts among Bitcoin addresses. Bitcoin balances are kept using public and private keys, long strings of numbers and letters linked through a mathematical encryption algorithm. The public key is like a bank account number and is the address to which others may send a user Bitcoins. The private key is like a password and is used to authorize transactions. Bitcoin transfers can be done with minimal processing fees, making it much cheaper for users to transfer money.

The idea of Bitcoin and digital currency is catching on. As of February 2016, there were 15.2 million Bitcoins in circulation. In addition, about 700 other cryptocurrencies have been created. Large financial institutions, such as JP Morgan Chase, have shown interest in digital currencies.

BLOCKCHAIN

At the heart of Bitcoin is its blockchain technology. A blockchain is an online, public ledger of all bitcoin transactions. With each new transaction, a completed

Blythe Masters, the chief executive officer of Digital Asset Holdings, speaks in an interview at the Singapore Fintech Conference in November 2016.

block is added to the blockchain. The blocks are added in a linear, chronological order. Each computer connected to the Bitcoin network that validates and relays transactions automatically receives a copy of the blockchain. The blockchain has the entire history of bitcoin transactions, from the first to the most recent. With countless numbers of blocks, the blockchain is a permanent database of bitcoin transactions. Each block is like an individual bank statement.

The blockchain database is shared by all computers participating in the system running Bitcoin software. Many experts believe that the blockchain technology may be able to be adapted for use in other technologies, such as online voting and crowdfunding.

MINING

As people send bitcoins to each other online, someone needs to keep a record of the transactions. The blockchain ledger is kept up to date by thousands of independently owned competing computers called miners. Bitcoin's developer turned the task of adding new transactions to the ledger into a competition known as mining. The mining process creates a secure transaction record, even though there is no central authority in charge of the digital currency.

When a person pays for something using Bitcoins, the transaction is immediately sent to the entire Bitcoin network. The parties use pseudonyms to keep their identities secret. The transaction is coded in alphanumeric data that does not reveal the user's personal identity. Bitcoin miners gather the digital information. They compete to turn the transaction into a block. The miner that successfully packages the data from the purchase adds it as a block to the blockchain ledger. The miner is rewarded with Bitcoins. About every ten minutes, a new block is added to the blockchain by mining. Every miner has a copy of the blockchain ledger. It can be used to prove ownership of Bitcoins.

The entire mining process takes about ten minutes to an hour. This is much shorter than the two-to three-day wait for the traditional settlement of a credit card transaction. In addition, there are virtually no fees and a user's personal information is not disclosed.

DIGITAL CURRENCY AND THE FUTURE

Bitcoins and other digital currencies are a completely new monetary system. They allow individual users to have more control over their money without the involvement of banks. Although these technologies are still very new, they are growing. Many companies offer Bitcoin exchange and payment services. More people are using Bitcoins to pay for goods and services. In addition, companies such as DELL, Overstock, and Expedia have started accepting Bitcoin payment on their websites.

Adam Ludwin, cofounder and chief executive of Chain, speaks at a conference in New York City in 2016 about Bitcoin and blockchain technology and applications.

Several companies have formed to support digital currencies and blockchain technology. Companies such as Chain are building software to help the financial industry replace existing record-keeping systems with blockchain technology. Chain's CEO, Adam Ludwin, believes that banks will eventually use the blockchain to transmit assets themselves, instead of just messages recording the transfer of assets. Chain has developed blockchain protocol for companies such as Visa and Capital One, along with other financial companies.

WORKING AS AN INFORMATION SECURITY ENGINEER

Security is major issue for many fintech platforms, including digital currency and blockchain technology. Digital security professionals are in high demand at fintech companies. These employees protect company computer network and systems, as well as design effective security features for fintech products.

Information security engineers typically monitor their company's networks for security breaches. If a suspected breach occurs, they investigate, resolve, and report it. These professionals also install and use security software such as firewalls and data encryption programs to protect company information. Security engineers will also perform testing on company systems to see if any vulnerabilities exist before a breach occurs. They stay informed about the latest developments in security technology and advise the company about cybersecurity matters. Many security engineers also work with others in the company to develop a security or disaster recovery system.

Security engineers may also lead a company's security efforts regarding online platforms and customer products. They advise the product and engineering teams on security and encryption protocol. They help engineering teams design secure software architecture. They also design and implement secure server configurations and developer machines. Some security engineers also act as the lead for external security audits.

DRAWBACKS TO DIGITAL CURRENCIES

Although digital currencies have many benefits, they also have some drawbacks. First, Bitcoins and other digital currencies are not legal tender anywhere in the world. Because they are not controlled by a central bank like the US dollar, the value of digital currencies can fluctuate wildly. Security is another concern. The software applications that manage Bitcoins have been vulnerable to hackers. There have been more than forty known thefts of Bitcoin wallets, with losses in the millions of dollars. And because users hide their identities with pseud-onyms, criminals may take advantage of the system and use digital currency to support illegal activity.

HOW TO BECOME AN INFORMATION SECURITY ENGINEER

Most information security engineers have at least a bachelor's degree in computer science, programming, or a related field. Some employers require a master of business administration (MBA) in information systems. Strong technical skills are essential, with employers looking for candidates with experience in Linus, C pro-gramming, Python, Perl, Shell, IP networks, firewalls, and routing methodology.

Many employers also look for candidates who have experience in a related job. Many get this experience by working in information technology departments, often in network or systems administration. In these jobs, they learn hands-on skills that they can use as security engineers. For example, if a job is related to database security, the company may look for a person who has experience as a database administrator.

Students wanting to work as security engineers may want to earn one or more information security certifications. Earning a certification shows that a person has the knowledge and best practices required for the job. Some certificates are general, while others are more specialized.

Two security engineers meet in the server room to examine computer equipment as they discuss a disaster recovery plan for the company's computer servers and networks.

In addition to strong technical skills, successful security engineers have several other qualities and skills. Information security engineers use problem-solving and analytical skills to study computer systems and networks to assess risks, discover weaknesses, and improve security procedures. Attention to detail is also important, as security engineers must be able to spot the tiniest breach in a company's digital security. Security engineers in the fintech industry should also have a knowledge of finance so that they can understand their company's and customers' needs. Security engineers should also have excellent communication and interpersonal skills. They often work as part of team and must be able to communicate effectively with team members, management, and others who may not have a technical background.

JOB OUTLOOK

The job outlook for security engineers is very good. According to the Bureau of Labor Statistics' *Occupational Outlook Handbook*, employment of information security analysts and engineers is projected to grow 18 percent from 2014 to 2024. This rate of growth is much faster than the average of all occupations. As more business is conducted online, cyberattacks and the theft of financial and personal information is a growing problem. Security engineers will be needed to find solutions to prevent hackers from stealing information or disrupting computer networks.

In fintech, the growing opportunities for security engineers are driven by the rapid increase in online platforms and services for consumers. As finance companies expand their online offerings, demand for security engineers will continue to increase. Candidates who have strong technical skills and related work experience will have the best opportunities for working as security engineers in the fintech industry.

CHAPTER SIX

THE FUTURE OF FINTECH CAREERS

From banking to personal finance, financial technologies are changing how the finance industry operates. Innovations such as algorithms for asset management, digital currencies, and peer-to-peer lending have sparked investment in numerous start-up companies. Even traditional finance and investment companies are embracing financial technology as a way to make their businesses more efficient and streamlined. "The speed and energy with which fintech innovation is impacting financial services is gathering global momentum," says Ian Pollari, global co-lead of accounting firm KPMG's fintech practice, according to Businesssbecause.com. Fintech is transforming the traditional financial business model. And the transformation is creating new opportunities for people who are looking to combine an interest in finance with computer science.

Almost every financial service offered by banks will soon be offered by a fintech company. Technology is creating better, faster, and less expensive services. It gives the average person more choices for his or her money and investments. Most experts predict that fintech will go more mainstream in the future. In a TransferWise report, 68 percent of people surveyed in 2015 said that they had never used a fintech company for financial services. In five years, almost half said that they expect to use fintech for at least one financial service. And in ten years, one-fifth of consumers predict that they will use technology companies for all financial services, from mortgages to credit cards.

TECH VS. FINANCE

According to industry experts, most fintech companies value technical skills over financial knowledge. While it is beneficial for a person to understand finance concepts, much of that knowledge can be learned on the job. According to Selby Jennings, a global recruitment firm that specializes in financial services, financial technology firms have realized that it is easier to train a smart tech employee on financial products than it is to teach a financial expert how to code. Tech companies are very fast-paced environments. Software releases and new services are introduced very quickly, and the margin for error is very small. As a result, tech-savvy employees who understand the complex programming and infrastructures are highly valued.

NEED FOR QUALIFIED PROFESSIONALS

The fintech industry is exciting and growing at a fast pace. As more entrepreneurs launch new start-up companies and existing fintech firms expand their operations, the industry will need to hire more qualified professionals. For students considering a career in fintech, the prospects of landing a job are very good.

The best opportunities will be available for people with solid computer science and financial skills. Some people enter fintech with a financial background,

Job seekers meet with representatives from companies and professional organizations at a career expo. This type of event gives participants the chance to talk to industry professionals.

while others bring a more technical, computer science background. Both are needed. Some people jump right into fintech, while others start out in traditional banking or financial institutions.

Arete Partners, a provider of executive search services specializing in the technology market, believes that fintech will continue to do well with global investment and increased hiring. Eoin O'Toole, Arete's cofounder and managing partner, says that his firm is seeing more fintech companies looking to hire. "While there isn't a perfect profile for the ideal candidate, we are seeing an increased demand for candidates with a solid knowledge of finance along with experience in the tech landscape. Financial experience is essential because of the complexity of economic markets and financial regulations. However, if someone has been working for a large financial institution for a long time, they may have a difficult time adjusting to the fast-paced environment of a tech start-up. So, there is an increasing demand for 'hybrid' candidates that have been on both sides of the desk," he says on the Arete Partners website.

AN EXCITING TIME FOR FINTECH

It is an exciting time in the fintech industry. The industry is projected to experience significant growth in the next few years. This growth is expected to create many opportunities for tech-savvy people who want to work in this field. For people who have an interest in both finance and computer science, a career in fintech may be the perfect fit.

GLOSSARY

algorithm A set of rules followed in a calculation or other problem-solving activity, often performed by a computer.

asset management The direction of a client's cash and investments by a financial services company.

biometric data Data that can be used to verify a person by his or her biological traits, such as a fingerprint or DNA.

credit rating An evaluation of the ability of a person to repay his or her debts.

crowdfunding The practice of raising money from a large number of people, usually over the internet.

cyberattack An attempt by hackers to destroy or damage a computer system or network.

data analytics The science of examining raw data and drawing conclusions from the information.

database A set of data held in a computer.

encryption A way of coding messages so that only authorized people can read them.

entrepreneur A person who starts, organizes, and operates a business.

equity Share in a public company.

funding Money or other financial resources.

innovation A new method, process, or product.

investor A person who provides money to a company in exchange for ownership.

personal finance The area of budgeting, saving, and investment for an individual or a family.

portfolio A range of investments held by a person or organization.

statistics A branch of math that deals with analyzing and interpreting data and numbers.

tokenization The process of substituting a sensitive data element with a nonsensitive equivalent.

web browser Software used to access pages on the internet.

web developer A programmer who specializes in development of the World Wide Web.

Association for Financial Technology
96 Northwoods Boulevard, Suite B2
Columbus, OH 43235
(614) 895-1208
Email: aft@aftweb.com
Website: http://aftweb.com/aws/AFT/pt/sp
    /home_page
The Association for Financial Technology (AFT) is a
    resource for networking and professional develop-
    ment for companies and executives in the fintech
    industry. The organization has members in virtu-
    ally every area of technology, data, or services in
    fintech.

Association of Software Professionals
ASP Executive Director
PO Box 1522
Martinsville, IN 46151
(765) 349-4740
Website: http://asp-software.org
The ASP is a professional trade association of soft-
    ware developers and provides a community for
    software developers to share information about the
    industry.

California Fintech Network
Website: http://www.californiafintech.org
The California Fintech Network is a nonprofit trade
    organization for people who work and invest in
    financial technology. Its website has links for

students, fintech company databases, job links, and more.

Digital Finance Institute
1500 - 885 West Georgia Street
Vancouver, BC V6C 3E8
Canada
(604) 601-2046
Email: admin@digitalfinanceinstitute.org
Website: http://www.digitalfinanceinstitute.org
The Digital Finance Institute is an organization that
   focuses on issues of financial innovations, digital
   finance policy and regulation, and women in the
   financial technology industry.

Fintech Professionals Association
(512) 981-7293
Email: info@fintechpros.org
Website: http://fintechpros.org
The Fintech Professionals Association works to bring
   the traditional financial services world together with
   new and emerging financial technology companies
   in order to share opportunities and ideas, and to
   network. The organization aims to create a vibrant
   online community of fintech professionals.

Information Technology Association of Canada
5090 Explorer Drive, Suite 510
Mississauga, ON L4W 4T9
Canada
(905) 602-8345
Website: http://itac.ca

The Information Technology Association of Canada supports the development of a digital economy in Canada. It represents information technology professionals in a wide variety of industries, including fintech.

WEBSITES

Because of the changing nature of internet links, Rosen Publishing has developed an online list of websites related to the subject of this book. This site is updated regularly. Please use this link to access the list:

http://www.rosenlinks.com/CYP/fintech

Abraham, Nikhil. *Coding for Dummies.* Hoboken, NJ: John Wiley & Sons, 2016.

Butler, Tamsen. *The Complete Guide to Personal Finance for Teenagers and College Students.* Ocala, FL: Atlantic Publishing, 2015.

Kassnoff, David. *What Degree Do I Need to Pursue a Career in Information Technology and Information Systems?* New York, NY: Rosen Publishing, 2014.

La Bella, Laura. *Building Apps.* New York, NY: Rosen Publishing, 2015.

Lowe, Doug. *Java All-in-One for Dummies.* Hoboken, NJ: John Wiley & Sons, 2014.

Matthes, Eric. *Python Crash Course: A Hands-On, Project-Based Introduction to Programming.* San Francisco, CA: No Starch Press, 2015.

Niver, Heather. *Careers for Tech Girls in Computer Science.* New York, NY: Rosen Publishing, 2014.

Peterson, Judy Monroe. *Smart Strategies for Investing Wisely and Successfully* (Financial Security and Life Success for Teens). New York, NY: Rosen Classroom, 2014.

Rosen Publishing. Code Power: A Teen Programmer's Guide (series). New York, NY: Rosen Publishing, 2015.

Spraul, V. Anton. *Think Like a Programmer: An Introduction to Creative Problem Solving.* San Francisco, CA: No Starch Press, 2012.

BIBLIOGRAPHY

Arete Partners. "Fintech Hiring to Remain Strong for Remainder of 2016." August 9, 2016. http://aretepartners.com/blog/fintech-hiring-remain-strong-remainder-2016.

Clarke, Paul. "Skills You'll Need to Work in Financial Technology." efinancialcareers.com. http://news.efinancialcareers.com/us-en/careers-in-finance/220773/fintech-skills.

FintechRanking.com. "15 Useful Personal Finance Management Services." March 18, 2016. http://fintechranking.com/2016/03/18/15-useful-personal-finance-management-services.

Fintech Valley. "Fintech Business Models—of Fintech Categories Part One." December 8, 2014. https://fintechvalley.org/2014/12/08/fintech-business-models-or-fintech-categories-part-one.

Fuscaldo, Donna. "The Rise of Fintech—What You Need to Know & Financial Services Now Offered." Goodcall.com. https://www.goodcall.com/personal-finance/fintech/#section5.

Henry, David. "U.S. Banks Add Pieces to New Instant Payments Network." Reuters.com. October 24, 2016. http://www.reuters.com/article/us-usa-banks-payments-idUSKCN1200BP.

Lesse, Katelyn. "Three Things I Learned in My Engineering Internship." Betterment.com. http://www.betterment.com/resources/inside-betterment/engineering/engineering-internship-betterment.

Moore, Michael. "Banks Must Make Digital Push as

Rivals Gain: McKinsey." Bloomberg.com. December 16, 2014. http://www.bloomberg.com/news /articles/2014-12-16/banks-must-make-digital -push-as-rivals-gain-mckinsey.

Murray, Seb. "Future of FinTech: Disruptive Startups Lure MBAs to Bitcoin, Peer-to-Peer Lending." BusinessBecause. February 22, 2016. http://www .businessbecause.com/news/future-of-fintech /3799/disruptive-fintech-startups-lure-mbas.

PricewaterhouseCoopers. "Peer Pressure: How Peer-to-Peer Lending Platforms Are Transforming the Consumer Lending Industry." February 2015. https://www.pwc.com/us/en/consumer-finance /publications/assets/peer-to-peer-lending.pdf.

Stahl, Lesley. "Fintech: Shaking Up the Financial Industry." CBS News.com. May 1, 2016. http:// www.cbsnews.com/news/fintech-shaking-up-the -financial-industry.

TechDay. "Why I Took a Break from Banking to Enroll in Coding Bootcamp." https://techdayhq.com/news /why-i-left-deustche-bank-to-learn-code.

Toren, Matthew. "10 Crowdfunding Success Stories to Love." Entrepreneur.com. March 18, 2014. https:// www.entrepreneur.com/article/232234.

INDEX

V

W

ABOUT THE AUTHOR

Carla Mooney is a graduate of the University of Pennsylvania. Before becoming an author, she spent several years working in finance as an accountant. Today, she writes for young people and is the author of many books for young adults and children. Mooney enjoys learning about new technologies and the impact they will have on the finance industry and the average consumer. She appreciates the convenience of financial technology and is looking forward to using more in the future.

PHOTO CREDITS

Cover ASDF_Media/Shutterstock.com; p. 1 (background) Verticalarray/Shutterstock.com; p. 3 (background) Toria/Shutterstock.com; pp. 5, 9, 15, 23, 56, 59 Bloomberg/Getty Images; p. 11 Frontpage/Shutterstock.com; p. 13 Thiago Leite/Shutterstock.com; p. 21 Roman Dementyev/Shutterstock.com; p. 25 © iStockphoto.com/Izabela Habur; p. 29 dot-shock/Shutterstock.com; p. 32 Don Emmert/AFP/Getty Images; p. 34 Mike Kemp/In Pictures/Getty Images; p. 36 © iStockphoto.com/PeopleImages; p. 39 michaeljung/Shutterstock.com; p. 43 I Believe I Can Fly/Shutterstock.com; p. 45 Syda Productions/Shutterstock.com; p. 48 Rawpixel.com/Shutterstock.com; p. 50 © iStockphoto.com/PointImages; pp. 54-55 Jack Guez/AFP/Getty Images; p. 62 Mark Agnor/Shutterstock.com; p. 67 Richard Levine/Corbis News/Getty Images; back cover, pp. 4-5 (background) nadla/E+/Getty Images; interior background pages graphics pp. 8, 20, 31, 42, 53, 65 (business graph) Johan Swanepoel/Shutterstock.com, (binary code) Titima Ongkantong/Shutterstock.com.

Designer: Michael Moy
Editor and Photo Researcher: Bethany Bryan